D0412028

When Hope and History Rhyme

The NUI, Galway
Millennium Lecture Series

When Hope and History Rhyme

The NUI, Galway
Millennium Lecture Series

Ruth Curtis

EDITOR

FOUR COURTS PRESS

Set in Adobe Garamond by
FOUR COURTS PRESS LTD
Fumbally Lane, Dublin 8, Ireland
e-mail: info@four-courts-press.ie
http://www.four-courts-press.ie
and in North America
FOUR COURTS PRESS
c/o ISBS, 5824 N.E. Hassalo Street, Portland, OR 97213.

A catalogue record for this title
is available from the British Library.

ISBN 1–85182–672–6

Printed in Ireland by
Betaprint Ltd, Dublin.

Contents

Acknowledgements

I AM VERY GRATEFUL to Seamus Heaney for allowing us to use his poetic words in the title of this book which encapsulates the spirit of the lectures. Grateful acknowledgement is made to Thomas Kinsella for the lines appearing on p. 65 taken from his poem 'Remembering Old Wars', first published as part of the sequence *Wormwood* (Dublin, 1966) and subsequently in *Collected Poems 1956–1994* (Oxford, 1996).

Special thanks are due to Mr Michael Sullivan, US Ambassador to Ireland (1999–2001), and to Fiona Bateman and Anne Whelan, NUI, Galway, for their editorial assistance with this publication.

Preface

It is with great pleasure that I introduce this fascinating series of lectures delivered in National University of Ireland, Galway in 1999, the year the University celebrated 150 years of student enrolment.

Sixty-eight students, all men, registered in this College in 1849 and thus began the dynamic intellectual and physical development of Queen's College Galway to University College Galway to National University of Ireland, Galway. Dr Patrick F. Fottrell, President, NUI, Galway (1996–2000), initiated these celebrations which inter alia included the restoration of the Quadrangle, the publication of a history of the University edited by Professor Tadhg Foley, and the commissioning of a large sculpture, *Twin Spires*, for the University grounds by internationally renowned sculptor John Behan.

The timing of our celebrations, which coincided with the new millennium, reminded us of the importance of the University as a place where significant issues are addressed and interrogated. The highlight of the celebrations, therefore, was the Millennium Lecture Series delivered by eminent individuals from different spheres of life. First Lady Hillary Rodham Clinton (now Senator of New York), UN High Commissioner for Human Rights, Mary Robinson, Senator George Mitchell, Nobel Laureate Seamus Heaney and Her Excellency President Mary McAleese accepted the University's invitation to participate in this forum. Each Millennium Lecture Series speaker was presented with a replica of Twin Spires by the University President.

Having such eminent and articulate people from Irish and

American society share their views with the University and with the wider community was intellectually stimulating. Each speaker palpably struck a chord with the different audiences as they presented their themes, moving from international to personal perspectives. They instilled within us a sense of reflection and realistic expectation facing into the new millennium. Their words and thoughts may now be accessed by a wider audience. I am very appreciative of the speakers' generous agreement to the publication of their Millennium Lectures.

Ruth Curtis
Vice-President for Development & External Affairs,
NUI, Galway

Our Obligations to Each Other: Continuing the Quest for Peace

First Lady Hillary Rodham Clinton

Here in Galway one must think of all those men and women and children who began their journey to what they called the 'New World' in ships sailing from this port. Some made America their home and became part of those immigrants who enriched, built and led our nation, and who now number forty million strong. As we watch from the United States and see the economic and cultural benefits that Ireland is celebrating today, it is a great joy. It is no wonder that so many Irish Americans and Irish living in America find their way back here – not only for a visit or retirement, but for investment and education – so that the bonds between us grow even stronger.

I know that this university opened its doors during the height of the potato famine. I know that your mission today remains as it has always been, that is, to teach and educate generations of young people, not only in the arts and the sciences, but in a timeless lesson about how we live with one another. What are the values we live by? How can we use our education to make a contribution, not only for our own personal success, but to the larger world as well?

We too, at the White House, have celebrated the millennium with a series of lectures, because we also believe that it is appropriate to mark this passage of time with some reflection.

We chose as our theme, 'Honour the past, imagine the future.' This theme has a lot of resonance not only in the United States, but here in Ireland and throughout the world. As we move into this new century and, indeed, this new millennium, many of us are asking ourselves, 'What are the ways we wish to bring with us? What are the values, the verities, which we do not want to lose in this passage to new time? Yet, also, what do we want to leave behind? What can we de-shackle ourselves from, give up? No longer let drag us down as we move forward?' These decisions require the imagination to see a future you wish to help create and also the courage to bring it about.

I wanted to talk today about our obligations to each other and the continuation of the quest for peace. It seems a particularly fitting and timely topic here on the island of Ireland, because we are in the middle of implementing the Accords. There is still great hope and optimism in the hearts and minds of people from one end of this island to the other. Yet we live in a time at the end of this century, when we know that peace is a challenge to us – how we realize it, and how we maintain it. We know, even as we speak today, that it is a challenge in the Balkans, in the Middle East, in parts of Africa and elsewhere. It seems that all of us, as we honor the past and imagine the future, have an opportunity to think harder about what our obligations are to one another and the obligations we all have to strive for peace.

Last month at the White House, we held the sixth in a series of interactive Millennium Lectures. Perhaps students or faculties here might have logged on, because they are cyber-cast simultaneously on the Internet – the first time that was ever done at the White House. The topic for this last lecture was the 'Perils of Indifference' and the speaker was the Nobel

Peace Prizewinner, Elie Wiesel. I had asked him to speak a year ago. I could not have known then what would be going on in the world today, but I knew at the time I asked him that the lessons of this too-violent century could not be forgotten, except at our peril. And I knew that his eloquence and his writing reminded all of us, year after year, how we cannot forget how we have to move forward into the uncertainties of hope.

Mr Wiesel came to that lecture in the midst of the NATO mission and reminded us of the terrible destruction and human suffering that has occurred in this century when evil has gone unchecked, and when the sacred bonds that should exist among human beings have been broken or ignored. He reminded us that those who stand by are not only bystanders, but are in danger of losing their own souls. He said that in concentration camps, there are only three kinds of people: killers, victims and bystanders. He said that we need to think hard about how we would avoid the perils of indifference.

At the end of his lecture, we had questions and answers from the audience. The last question was from a Catholic priest who teaches at Georgetown University. He asked Mr Wiesel, in the light of what he had personally suffered as a young boy – whisked from his home in Romania, put into a concentration camp, losing most of his family – how he could look to the future with any hope whatsoever. Well, he stood back for a minute and he said: 'But what is our alternative? We either give in to the evil and the indifference, or we constantly nurture hope in ourselves and those who come after us.'

This past century has taught us that hope is the only answer. Economic and social progress is possible only when people of different backgrounds, experiences and traditions let go of the past, let go of old hatreds, and decide that their common human obligations and potential common future offer greater promise than either indifference or antipathy.

It has always been true, but certainly I think – given the situation in the world today with the spread of weapons of mass destruction, and once again conflicts among peoples and religions and tribes – that we all have a role to play in the continuing quest for peace. Peace will more than ever depend on what each of us does and whether we can overcome our past on behalf of a common future.

Another Nobel Prize winner, Seamus Heaney, wrote something that became the guiding hope for my husband and I on our many visits to Ireland and, much more than that, in our work around the world as well. Some of you may remember that during the President's 1995 visit, he quoted from a wonderful passage that became the hallmark of why we believe hope has to be our goal. Let me remind you of those lines:

> History says, don't hope on this side of the grave. But then, once in a lifetime, the longed for tidal wave of justice can rise up, and hope and history rhyme.

Reading that, or listening to Elie Wiesel, we know that the great forces of history and the great evil that lurks in the cold regions of the human soul are formidable. But there is not just a possibility but a necessity for all of us to work to ensure that hope and history rhyme.

Since I first visited Northern Ireland with the President in November of 1995, I have seen with my own eyes how far people have moved from history to hope. I've seen it in the important agreements that have been reached. I've seen it in the handshakes and conversations of political leaders. I've seen it in the economic growth that holds out promise for prosperity. Yes, the guns that have been silenced, the prisoners that have been released, and the election of a truly representative Assembly – all are fulfilling a promise of the Good Friday Agreement.

But more than that, I have seen it in small ways. Yes we have needed and we will always need courageous leaders who are willing to take risks for peace; but more than even leaders, we will need men and women who can change their hearts – young and old, Protestant and Catholic, and in other parts of the world as well. Here the people knew it was time to end the bloodshed, to stop the hatred and violence, to do better for our children. So in both the North and the South they set about doing the everyday work of peace – in their homes, their schools, their workplaces, and their communities. It is citizens like these who have raised their voices and used their votes, who are moving this entire island and history to hope, from war to peace, and from the past to the future.

There are some who criticize the United States because we often seem to lack a sense of history. Very often the history we have has been given a makeover, so that we find room for everyone at the table. We have had some very hard times in our own history, when we have had to fight a civil war, had to confront discrimination and bigotry against all kinds of people – against the Irish, against the Blacks, against the Hispanics, against women – all kinds of people. But slowly and surely we have moved from our history to hope. It is probably one of the hallmarks of the American experience that sometimes seems naive and even a little bit silly to those looking at us from outside our shores: this sense of possibility, this unrealistic hope in the face of reality. Yet it has served us very well.

America is an idea that is rooted in hope, potential, possibility and promise and because of that, we've been able to move beyond our history. Therefore, it is difficult sometimes for an American visiting anywhere else in the world, where the grip of history seems so strong and people seem to be struggling and dying under it, to understand why that grip cannot be broken. It seems that the values of the past that are good and hopeful and promising can be carried forward, so why can't those, which drag us back, be left behind?

All over the world I have met people who have seen of the worst of what human beings are capable of and who have summoned up the best of their humanity to bring peace and dignity to all. I have sat at tables with people who were combatants – one against the other in Central America, in El Salvador and Guatemala – who have seen, only recently, the ending of decades of bloodshed and conflict. I have listened as one guerilla leader said to a political leader who was then on the other side, 'We never thought we could trust you. The hardest thing in the world for us was signing the peace agreement that included disarmament, but we knew finally the time had come; we had to move forward.'

I have seen the commitment in the Middle East, where so much blood has been shed and where so much distrust still lingers. I have listened to how Christians, Jews and Muslims have struggled to find some agreement with one another, yet have been willing to lay down the burdens of the past for the promise of a hopeful future. During the last visit that my husband and I made, I visited a small community in Israel, where Christians, Jews and Muslims had made a conscious effort to live together side by side, to respect each other's traditions, to try to serve as an example for their fellow men and women. I watched three small children celebrate their own traditions.

One lit a Christmas tree, one a menorah, the third a Ramadan lamp. Each was celebrating his or her own faith and learning how religion can be a source of strength and hope, not divisiveness.

Shortly after the Dayton Peace Accords, I was in Bosnia. In Tuzla I met a predominantly female group of Orthodox Christians, Catholic Christians, Muslims, and even a Jew, all of whom had survived the horrific onslaught of ethnic cleansing. They told me what that experience had been like, how each had fought to survive, how they had tried to keep a normal life going: keeping some remnant of schooling available in a basement; trying to keep a hospital functioning despite the lack of supplies; moving from house to house, corner to corner, avoiding the bombs and the guns. They gave me a small statue of a woman, carved of wood. Embedded in her knee is a piece of shrapnel that had been picked up from the street, a symbol certainly of the war and the pain that had been endured; but her hand is on her heart and, on her other hand, a dove of peace. She has a confident smile that seems to say, 'I will dream again; I will work for peace for my children.' Some might say that I am being sentimental; that this is the kind of dream that is unrealistic, given what we know about the world. Yet I would argue that we should always hope for the best while being prepared for the worst; these are not contradictory. We know what lurks in the human soul, we know of what men and women are capable, but if we don't believe that it can be better, then we perpetuate the cycle of violence, disappointment and indifference.

I want to commend all of you here in Ireland for the work that your country has done on behalf of peacekeeping. Irish peacekeepers have been in Bosnia, the Congo, Lebanon and many other places around the world. I know that you have just received your first Kosovo refugees, and that you are offering them your hearts and your homes, as you always have done. These refugees are stark reminders, if we needed any, of how far we have yet to go at the end of this century. When communism fell in the Soviet Union and we all celebrated the physical destruction of the Berlin Wall, who could have predicted, that only ten years later, we would be faced again with the kind of violence, oppression and evil that we see emanating from Yugoslavia?

I met the first group of refugees who came to the United States last week. There were grandmothers in shawls, there were students who spoke perfect English, there were children running around, and there was even a woman who was on the verge of giving birth. As I looked into their eyes, particularly the children's, I tried to imagine what they had witnessed and endured. We have only seen the pictures: the haunting images of children crowded in the trains, robbed of their homes, their families, their childhood.

I was talking with our aid workers and they told me just a few stories that they personally had experienced in a refugee camp. Seeing a woman surrounded by small children sobbing uncontrollably, they asked her if there was anything that could be done for her. In an attempt to make conversation, the worker said, 'Well, at least you have your children with you.' Then the woman began to cry harder, because, as they were herded into these trains, they were pushed apart and she had lost three of her children. She had no idea where they were. We, at the Embassy, were able to locate them. I think to any parent, who sometimes can become somewhat immune to the pictures on television, the suffering seems too much. It seems so far away, we are not sure what we can do. To translate it into those personal terms of a mother losing her children makes it all too real. Despite the suffering that they had endured, the refugees I met wanted, more than anything, to return home and to begin rebuilding their lives in peace and safety. That is the goal and the mission the United States and NATO have undertaken. It is also a reminder that, basically, that is what most people want. They want to be left alone, to be able to raise their families, to have the joys that come in life; and too often, the reality is that they have been prohibited from doing so.

As we enter this new millennium, people all over the world are looking to this island. We know how deep the bitterness has run. We know how important it is that progress continues. And we look to the people here, in both the North and the South, to teach us what enduring peace looks like. Not just the absence of conflict, but the presence of justice – that tidal wave of justice that can rise up. We know that justice can only rise up when citizens have access to the tools of opportunity, like quality education, healthcare, jobs and credit; when they can make their voices heard in a political system; and when they all feel that they have a stake in the future that we want everyone to participate in building. We know that justice can only rise up if all people are welcome in the decision-making processes of governments, of business, of academia, of every institution.

I have a particular admiration for the women of the North who have worked for years throughout the Troubles to bring people together. Eight months ago I was privileged to launch the 'Vital Voices: Women in Democracy' conference in Belfast. I will return tomorrow for a follow-up teleconference. Women, members of both traditions, had come from all over this island. Some were experienced activists; some had never done anything in public before. One who introduced me was a student, aged fifteen or so. 'It was the first time', one woman said to me, 'that we realized a sense of possibility. We realized we could be the architects of a new Northern Ireland.' Indeed they can, and they are.

When I meet again with them tomorrow, I will be hearing about the progress that has been made since our last meeting in September. I will be hearing about the partnerships, some of them involving American companies and organizations, that are working to build services in communities and assist women and others who are starting new businesses and strengthening their leadership and advocacy skills. Because the hard work of peace – again, only when the accords are signed, whether it is the Dayton Accords in Bosnia which ended the violence and created the conditions for peace there, or whether it is the Good Friday Accord here – the hard work of peace is what each of us does every day.

What I have seen is that hard work of peace taking place here. I have heard about it. I have watched it not be derailed, as some continue to resort to violence to try to disrupt and end the quest for peace. At the Vital Voices conference, I met a young woman who had lost friends in the Omagh bombing. One of her best friends was killed. When she was called and invited to come as one of the student representatives to the Vital Voices conference, her mother was not sure how she would feel about it, because it might be considered political. She was in no mood for politics. Yet this young woman came because she wanted to be part of the quest for peace. She knew she had to make a contribution.

This is what you are working to create here at this university, not only by educating and informing young people about their obligations, but in particular through the work of the Irish Centre for Human Rights. You understand that justice

can only rise up when the everyday lessons of peace and freedom and mutual respect are learnt by every generation.

To assist you in your work, I am pleased to announce a
new partnership. The Irish government has agreed to join the
American philanthropic foundation, the Ferris Foundation,
to create ten scholarships for outstanding African-American
graduate students to study at colleges in the North and South
of Ireland, including here in Galway. You understand how
important it is for people to live and work and learn together.
I am also told that a group called Cooperation Ireland is help-
ing to build trust and friendships between Catholic and
Protestant children by organizing exchanges across the border.
Children who lived only a few miles from each other, but have
never met, are now visiting each other's schools and staying in
each other's homes.

At the Vital Voices conference, I was struck by how little
real contact existed between people in the North. Women,
with some amazement, learned that they had the same feelings and experiences. They were all worried when their children went out to play, or when their husbands went off to
work. They all prayed to the same God on Sunday to make
sure they would come home safely. As they began to appreciate their common experience, trust began to grow.

I hope that the work – the hard work – of peace, based on
our sense of obligation and our commitment to the future,
will have the support of all people who understand how
important it is that we get on the right side of history so that
hope and history might rise.

I imagine that at the end of the next century, students and
faculties of this university may be coming together in a setting
like this, or more likely a virtual meeting. The purpose would
be the same. They also will want to know what else they need

to do to keep moving from history to hope. I trust that when that meeting is held we will have given them a century of better news that the one we leave behind. I trust that we will have taught them that for each generation there is the work of peace, and that it is not an easy task. It is not enough to take a vote or pass a law; each of us has to struggle every single day. Only individuals can decide whether we are going to love or hate, whether we will respect one another or whether we will use our superficial differences – be they skin colour or religious faith or gender or any other distinguishing characteristics of the human family – as reason enough to treat someone as less than human. Only individuals can decide whether we will expand the circle of human dignity to all those who are unlike ourselves. Only we can stay true to our obligations.

My husband received a letter from a family that had lost a loved one in the bombing in Omagh. This man wrote to my husband because he knew he was a father like Bill is. He wrote about his hopes for his daughter who had been newly born. This is what he said: 'We have a dream of what Ireland might be like when she grows up. Ireland could be a place where dreams could come true, where people would achieve things never imagined before, where people would not be afraid of their neighbours.'

I go from here to Belfast to help dedicate a park. It is a park where we hope that children of both traditions will play in safety and joy together. We asked the children themselves to design this playground. And what did they dream of? They dreamed of tree houses and birdhouses. They want to have a footbridge and a maze constructed from bushes. They want an area to plant things in. They dream what all of us dream of – a chance just to be safe, to laugh, to love, to play. I hope that patch of soil will be a symbol of what is possible and that all of us will look toward the future together.

I hope that I can come back and see that playground in years to come and watch children playing without fear or prejudice, learning to solve their problems without violence. And when they grow up and leave that playground, knowing that they will become architects of their community, that they will be committed also to ensuring that their children play in peace, and that justice is always rising up, and that hope and history rise.

Thank you for what you are doing to make peace real, to make the quest for peace the responsibility and obligation of us all. Thank you for the example that this island is setting. I trust and I pray the example will stand far, far into the future as the kind of commitment that we all will be called to meet.

12 May 1999

Human Rights at the Dawn of the New Millennium

Mary Robinson, United Nations High Commissioner for Human Rights

This is a good time to take stock of what has been achieved in defining and promoting human rights in the world. Last year saw the fiftieth anniversary of the Universal Declaration of Human Rights. This year is the tenth anniversary of the International Convention on the Rights of the Child. Now, as we embark on a new millennium where new issues and experiences await us, all we know for certain is that the struggle to protect human rights will go on. We have only achieved a fraction of what ought to have been achieved and the scene is constantly changing, throwing up new challenges which need to be addressed.

There is a more sombre reason why the issue of human rights is so topical at the moment, as we witness each day that, despite greater public acceptance of the concept and principles of human rights, gross abuses are still widespread.

I would like to share with you two recent experiences which, I think, throw light on the nature of the challenges we face in the human rights field. The first was the annual meeting of the United Nations Commission on Human Rights which ended three weeks ago, the second my recent visit to the Former Yugoslavia.

Commission on Human Rights

The main intergovernmental policy-making body concerned with human rights is the Commission on Human Rights. It meets for six weeks each year from the middle of March until the end of April. Fifty-three of the UN's member States are elected for a three-year period to serve on the Commission. A further eighty-nine States sent representatives as observers this year, as did most of the UN family of organizations and other international institutions. There was an active, lively presence on the part of non-governmental organizations or NGOs.

Ireland is currently a member of the Commission on Human Rights, having been elected in 1996. The chair of this year's Commission was Ireland's Ambassador to the United Nations in Geneva, Anne Anderson. Ambassador Anderson carried out her difficult duties with great skill and aplomb and her success in steering the Commission through consideration of issues that were often very complex drew praise from all sides for her personally and earned great credit for Ireland.

The Commission considers the situation in individual countries and debates the issues that currently make up the human rights agenda. A wide range of countries were looked at this year including Afghanistan, Burundi, Cuba, China, the Democratic Republic of Congo, the occupied Arab territories including Palestine, Sudan, Cambodia, and Colombia.

Issues discussed ranged from the rights of the child to the death penalty, from the impact of globalization to racial discrimination. Two topics, which were the subject of intense negotiation, were a revolution on Islam and one on measures to rationalize and improve the Commission's mechanisms. It was only at the eleventh hour that agreed texts were concluded on these two issues.

As is natural at such a large gathering of representatives of States, multilateral organizations and NGOs, the level of debate varied and the outcome under some of the different headings was not always what I would have hoped. To an outsider, the debate on some issues might appear abstruse and far removed from the real life abuses of human rights which happen every day around the world. And for some States the idea of their human rights performance being scrutinized and monitored remains unacceptable.

But the Commission plays a vital role in the continuing discussion about how all of us, and especially the United Nations, can and should approach human rights issues. For me and my colleagues it is a highly important channel which brings the concerns of the member States of the United Nations to our attention.

Not only that, but the Commission's resolutions provide legislative mandates for further work and play a major role in the shape and scope of my Office's activities. Two positive results this year were the useful discussions to prepare for the holding of the World Conference on Racism in 2001 and the dialogue on children which focused on practical ways to implement the Convention on the Rights of the Child globally.

Former Yugoslavia

I was conscious that this year's meeting of the Commission on Human Rights coincided with what has become the worst conflict on the European continent since the Second World War and the scene of the grossest abuses of human rights in recent times. With that in mind, I identified the issue of addressing violations of human rights during conflicts as a key issue for the Commission.

As the session got underway the full extent of ethnic cleansing in Kosovo began to be apparent. NATO's bombing campaign also intensified during this period. I therefore arranged that I would make regular reports to the Commission on the situation in the Former Yugoslavia. I made four such reports and issued two public statements while the Commission sat, drawing on information from personnel of my Office on the ground and in Geneva, from institutional partners, and from the Governments involved.

My objective was to bring to attention the issues of principle involved. I described these in my closing remarks as being fourfold:

- The principle of justice: that those responsible for ethnic cleansing be brought to justice.

- The principle of human rights protection: we must vindicate the rights of those who have been driven out to return to their homes and be compensated for losses and damage they have suffered.

- The principle of proportionality: the human cost of the bombing must be taken into account; the response to violent abuse of human rights must not entail more human rights violations.

- The principle of legality: the United Nations and the Security Council are the appropriate vehicle for determining our response to the Kosovo crisis.

I am more than ever convinced, after the events that have taken place since the end of April, that these four principles are essential to the conclusion of a lasting settlement of the Kosovo crisis and that the emphasis must be placed on an urgent search for a diplomatic solution.

Immediately after the Commission ended, I went to the Former Yugoslavia to see the situation on the ground for myself and to co-ordinate the monitoring and documenting of human rights violations. The contrast between the reasoned debate conducted in the Palais des Nations by delegates who, whatever their differences, follow strict rules of procedure and have signed up to certain standards and norms, and the scenes I witnessed in the following days was, as you can imagine, extraordinary. Aid workers are making a valiant effort to look after the hundreds of thousands of children, women and men who crowd the transit camps across Kosovo's borders. But the scale of the disaster is huge. The countries which are bearing the brunt of this enormous burden – Albania and the Former Yugoslav Republic of Macedonia – are having their scarce resources stretched well beyond their limit. They need help urgently and the international community should respond to the pressing needs immediately, before an even greater tragedy develops.

As always, it was the human face of what was to be seen in the camps that was the most affecting: women with horrible tales of rape and abuse, wracked by fear for their menfolk who have disappeared; children whose lives have been turned upside down overnight and who have no idea what the future holds. The confusion and trauma of elderly people, who had been driven from their homes and then seen those homes burn behind them, was heartbreaking to witness. And these scenes are happening in Europe, just a few hundred miles away from us.

A meeting was scheduled with President Milosevic but he chose not to meet me. I would like to have spoken to him. I would have told him of the eyewitness accounts I received which put beyond doubt that vicious human rights abuses have taken and still are taking place in Kosovo. I would have told him that these gross violations are being carried out by security forces under his command and in his name. I would have said that a grave responsibility rests with those who carry out such atrocities but an even graver responsibility rests with those who command and direct them.

A Challenge to Human Rights

The terrible events in Kosovo pose a direct challenge to all those involved in defending human rights values. The contrast between discussions about the nature of human rights such as those at the Commission in Geneva and the scenes I witnessed and reports I heard in the camps around Kosovo, underline the dilemma we face when we compare the theory and principles of human rights with the reality of what is happening around us.

And Kosovo, regrettably, is far from unique. Before that there was Bosnia. Genocide has taken place in Cambodia and Rwanda. A war is raging between Ethiopia and Eritrea, a war which has cost hundreds of lives. The human rights situation in East Timor is critical. There are reports of large-scale abuses in Sierra Leone.

One thing is certain: if we are to be serious about promoting and defending human rights, the message must go out that there can be no impunity for such crimes. Human rights monitors from my Office are already in the region working with international partners, including the International Criminal Tribunal for the Former Yugoslavia, to establish accountability and to ensure that the crimes being committed do not go unpunished. The guilty, whether in Former Yugoslavia or anywhere else in the world, must be made to see that they cannot escape the consequences of their actions.

Other Human Rights Abuses in the World

So far I have emphasized gross human rights abuses. That is because they stand out so blatantly before us. The thirty articles of the Universal Declaration of Human Rights cover a wide range of rights including the right to freedom of movement, to freedom of thought, religion and conscience, to a fair trial, to free assembly. These rights, too, are routinely denied in many parts of the world.

There is a further set of rights incorporated in the Universal Declaration – economic, social and cultural rights. They include the right to work, the right to equal pay for equal work, the right to food, clothing, housing and medical care. Many people, especially those living in poorer countries, feel that these economic, social and cultural rights have not received their proper share of attention. I think that this is a valid argument and one of my objectives has been to place more emphasis on these rights. Resource rich countries must pay greater attention to the economic and social rights of the marginalized members of their own societies and to the acute needs of developing countries. The gap between rich and poor is widening all the time and there is a tendency on the part of rich nations to give up on the developing countries. As well as being morally indefensible, such an attitude will lead to dangerous instability in the world.

Nor should we in Ireland feel complacent about our record in securing the rights enshrined in the Universal Declaration of Human Rights. For example, last week the UN Committee on Economic, Social and Cultural Rights issued a report on Ireland which showed that we have a long way to go. Among the criticisms in the report were the persistence of poverty among disadvantaged and vulnerable groups, the absence of appropriate legislation dealing with the rights of the mentally handicapped, the absence of specific legislation to deal with the rights of the physically disabled, our high levels of illiteracy, discrimination against the Travelling community and long waiting lists for medical services. The report also regretted that Ireland has not yet ratified the International Convention on the Elimination of all Forms of Racial Discrimination.

A Coalition for Human Rights

The challenge of embedding a culture of human rights in the world is formidable. It will not be achieved easily or quickly and there will be many setbacks on the way. The full co-operation of all the actors involved will be essential to achieve success. I would like to see a coalition of these actors – governments, international institutions, non-governmental organisations, the business community working together to achieve the goal of universal human rights.

Role of the High Commissioner for Human Rights

My Office must give the lead in the fight for human rights. The position I hold, as United Nations High Commissioner for Human Rights, is the most recently created of such posts in the UN system. It was established following the World Conference on Human Rights, held in Vienna in 1993. After eighteen months in the job, I have a clear understanding of the importance of the office and of the size of the task. The challenge is to convey a coherent philosophy of human rights and to back that with actions and services which function effectively.

The legal base is there. Real progress has been made in this century on the codification of international human rights law. The progress is all the more remarkable when it is remembered that the concept of internationally agreed principles of human rights is a relatively recent phenomenon. The Universal Declaration of Human Rights only took shape after the Second World War, while the two International Covenants that derive from it, on Civil and Political Rights, and on Economic, Social and Cultural Rights, are of more recent vintage. They were adopted by the General Assembly in 1966 and entered into force a decade later.

Over sixty human rights treaties have been concluded which elaborate the fundamental rights and freedoms contained in the International Bill of Rights. The four principal ones deal with racial discrimination; discrimination against women; torture and other cruel, inhuman or degrading treatment or punishment; and the rights of the child. In addition, there are many important Declarations on issues such as the Rights of Persons belonging to National or Ethnic Religions and Linguistic Minorities; Indigenous People; and the Elimination of Violence against Women.

The mechanisms to monitor adherence to these conventions and to investigate reports of abuses are improving. There are the so-called conventional mechanisms which monitor government's performance – for example, the Human Rights Committee which looks at adherence to the International Covenant on Civil and Political Rights; and the Committee on Economic, Social and Cultural Rights which monitors implementation of the second Covenant.

There are also what are referred to as Special Procedures which the Commission on Human Rights has at its disposal. These are more flexible arrangements than the ones that I've just mentioned. Special Rapporteurs are appointed to investigate the human rights situation in specific countries. There are also Special Rapporteurs who pursue a thematic mandate such as torture, religious intolerance or violence against women. The number of Special Rapporteurs has grown rapidly in recent years, in response to the demand for action in the case of gross human rights abuses. They make recommendations and are a very valuable instrument in the work of promoting human rights. A part of me rejoices when another Special Rapporteur is appointed since I know that a qualified expert will investigate specific abuses; another part of me wonders where the funding will come from!

Two valuable instruments at the disposal of my Office are Field Operations and Technical Co-operation Programmes. The first field presence was established in 1992; today there are twenty-two. The number of technical assistance programmes, which aim to assist countries in setting up their own human rights commissions and strengthen the culture of human rights, is also growing rapidly.

A most significant development was the decision last year to create an International Criminal Court. The decision represents a major breakthrough by governments to end the cycle of impunity and establish individual criminal responsibility. I urge States to ratify the Rome Statute so that the Court can begin its task. That task is the same as the job of any national criminal court: to prosecute, to educate, to punish and to deter.

I would be the first to admit that we have a long way to go before we can feel that the mechanisms are working as they should. Securing adequate funding for our operations is a time-consuming aspect of the job. It has helped that the Secretary General of the United Nations, Kofi Annan, undertook to place human rights at the heart of the work of the United Nations, as part of his reform of the organization.

For my part, I will do all in my power both to be a voice for those whose rights are denied or abused and will ensure that the mechanisms operated by my Office deliver the best possible results.

Role of Governments

Governments wield considerable influence in the human rights field, both for good and for ill. A heartening fact is that the large majority of governments now accept that they have human rights obligations. Those who argue that human rights are an internal affair are in a small minority. In practice, though, many governments continue to violate their citizens' rights, often under the pretext of protecting national security.

My chief approach to governments is one of dialogue and encouragement. If better results can be achieved through behind-the-scenes discussion, then I am happy to do that. Moral exhortation may well be the strongest weapon at my disposal, but I will not hesitate to speak out publicly and loudly when governments persist in abusing the rights of their citizens. That applies whether it is Yugoslavia or Burma, Afghanistan or Indonesia.

Prevention is central to my approach to dealing with governments. Prevention is the chief rationale of the field presence which my Office maintains and the technical co-operation programmes we are engaged in. The good news is that we are registering some significant successes in the field of prevention, even in countries where human rights have traditionally had shallow roots.

One effective way of getting in early to prevent and check on human rights breaches is effective National Human Rights Institutions. Such institutions are a valuable tool in instilling a culture of respect for rights in societies. A National Human Rights Institution can confer a sense of ownership and empowerment. It can resolve rights issues without the parties concerned having to resort to litigation.

I was delighted to see that Human Rights Institutions were to be set up both in Ireland and Northern Ireland as part of the Good Friday Agreement. It seems to me that, in post-conflict situations, national human rights institutions are particularly needed so as to restore the principles and practice of human rights and to promote reconciliation. The Northern Ireland Commission has already been set up. I have high hopes for the contribution it can make to this most sensitive stage of the peace process. It will, of course, be judged on its performance. It is my profound hope that it will be an effective instrument and hence play a central part in the peace process.

My Office has been advising the government here about the workings and remit of our National Human Rights Commission. I have urged that its powers should comply fully with what are called the Paris Principles, the norms seen as fundamental to such national commissions, and that it be given a mandate to investigate individual problems and, where possible, resolve them.

Regional co-operation is another interesting and often fruitful way to strengthen human rights. It enables governments to build on the experience and best practice of countries in their region, to co-operate with their neighbours and to use available resources in the most efficient way. The European and inter-American examples are especially effective. And, on my recent visits to India and to the first OAU Ministerial Conference on Human Rights in Mauritius, I have seen the value of this type of co-operation at firsthand.

Non-State Actors

Governments retain formidable powers but the role of non-State actors is steadily increasing. Big business is, in many respects, as powerful as national governments and in certain ways can be even more powerful. Building alliances with business is a high priority for me. Progress is being made in that the corporate sector is coming to realize that human rights are their business too and that their responsibilities are great. They are slowly but surely seeing the value of establishing benchmarks, promoting best practice and adopting meaningful codes of conduct. They are recognizing that a strong human rights culture is closely linked to national stability,

international security and a climate conducive to the success-
ful conduct of business.

International financial and developmental institutions
have a duty to ensure that their programmes take full account
of the human rights dimension. Policies of organizations such
as the IMF and the World Bank have far-reaching human
consequences. Too often responsibility for these consequences
is seen as belonging to someone other than the financial institutions. But it is their responsibility, and they should take
greater account of this aspect. A rights-based approach is by
far the likeliest way to achieve sustainable development.

The growth of non-governmental organizations or NGOs
is a positive development. NGOs are proliferating all over the
world – even in places where the concept is very new. The
spirit that I find when I meet NGO representatives is positive
and exciting. By working together in NGOs people are find-
ing their voice and feeling the freedom and empowerment
which comes from being able to influence the processes that
shape their lives.

Conclusion: The Role of the Individual

The coalition for human rights, which I would like to see, will
face many challenges as we enter the next millennium. In
addition to the traditional problems in the human rights field
there will be new issues to face. I think of such issues as genetic engineering and cloning, the genetic modification of food,
the environmental dimension of human rights and the
euthanasia debate which will undoubtedly grow in volume as
science's capacity to prolong human life increases. We will

need the active participation of all the actors involved if we are to hope to rise to the challenge.

One category I have not mentioned is the individual. In some ways the individual is the key to our future capacity to defend human rights. Every one of the actors to which I have referred – be it States, NGOs, the financial institutions or big business – is, after all, only a group of individuals acting together for a common purpose. Individuals can and do make an enormous difference in the fight for human rights. That is shown by the lengths to which oppressive governments and opponents of human rights will go to silence human rights defenders. We have seen this in Northern Ireland with the cowardly murder of Rosemary Nelson, killed because she was such a resolute champion of the rights of her community. One of the ablest of the liberal politicians in Russia, Galina Starovoitova, was murdered not long ago in St Petersburg. And last month we witnessed the pain of Aung Sung Suu Kyi, unable to be with her dying husband because of her fight to defend the rights of the Burmese people.

There are stories of triumph too, and none greater than that of Nelson Mandela. He has now entered a joyful and well-deserved retirement. When the history of South Africa is written it will be apparent how much his country and the world owes to Nelson Mandela. Dignified, wise and, above all, courageous, he is the embodiment of the truth that it is not those who inflict the most but those who endure the most who will prevail. It is small wonder that Nelson Mandela is one of the world's most respected champions of human rights, especially among the young.

How do individuals see the future of human rights as we approach the year 2000? To judge from the letters and e-mails I receive, with a good deal of apprehension and pessimism.

One of the things frequently said to me is: 'Your job is impossible. Human rights may make some advances in some places for some time but then mankind reverts to its old habits.' The kinder ones say: 'You are doing a good job and we admire you but it's a case of mission impossible.'

Needless to say, I don't share that view. To my mind, for any well-meaning person there is no choice: we must be on the side of human rights and what is more, we must each play our part to defend them. It is not true that the individual is powerless in the face of human rights abuses. We do have the capacity to make things change – so long as we choose to exercise it. We can speak up about abuses, galvanise support for worthwhile causes, and pressurise those in authority to accept their responsibilities. A practical example of how we in Ireland can play our part for human rights is the welcome we extend to refugees from the conflict in Kosovo. There was an opinion poll in a Sunday newspaper which said that half the people canvassed felt that Ireland had done enough by taking in a thousand refugees. Are we really so complacent and selfish that we cannot find room for more of those caught up in this awful conflict? I cannot believe that we have so abandoned our traditional instincts of open-heartedness and welcome, especially at a time when we are enjoying prosperity on a scale never experienced in Ireland before. Adopting a welcoming approach to these refugees would send a strong signal of our revulsion against the assault on their rights, which has put them in their present tragic situation.

Individuals can work together with the rest of the actors in the human rights scene and be a formidable voice for progress. As we approach the new millennium we should rededicate ourselves to achieving the dream of those who framed the Universal Declaration of Human Rights. They drew up that visionary document in the shadow of the Holocaust: it was born out of a determination that such horrors should not darken the face of the earth again. We will live up to their vision if we carry forward the task of translating the high ideals enshrined in the Universal Declaration into actions that serve to proclaim, champion and defend human rights.

20 May 1999

Making Peace

US Senator George Mitchell

In the year since the agreement was reached on Good Friday and approved in referendum and I returned to the United States, I travelled around the country and spoke to groups everywhere. Of the many questions I was asked, two repeated themselves over and over again: 'Is it really true, will there be peace in Northern Ireland?' and, secondly: 'Are there any lessons from Northern Ireland which may be useful in other conflicts?' This was asked, of course, most often during the recent months of the conflict in the Balkans. I'll begin with the second question and in the process get to the first. I think we must answer the question about lessons for other conflicts with great caution. Each society is different, each conflict is unique and while there are some common threads that run through them all, there are also different circumstances. Much as we would like it, there is not, in my view, any magic formula, which, once discovered, can be applied to conflicts wherever they occur. But there are, I believe, certain principles which have long held and which for me were validated by my experience in Northern Ireland.

First, I believe there is no such thing as a conflict that cannot be ended. Conflicts are created and sustained by human beings; they can be ended by human beings, no matter how ancient, no matter how hurtful, no matter how much damage has been done, conflict can be ended. When I arrived in Northern Ireland, just about four and a half years ago, I found to my dismay, a widespread feeling of pessimism among the people and the political leaders. As all of you know, it's a small and well-informed society. I quickly became well-known and every day, in a restaurant, on the street, in the airport or in a hotel lobby, people stopped me by the dozens and then the hundreds. They always began with kind words, 'Thank you Senator, God bless you Senator, we appreciate what you're trying to do,' but they always ended in despair, 'You're wasting your time, this conflict can't be solved, we've been killing each other for centuries and we're doomed to go on killing each other forever.' As best I could, I worked to reverse such attitudes. That's the special responsibility of political leaders from whom many of the public take their cue and after whom they pattern their own opinions. Leaders must lead and one way is to create an attitude of success – the belief that problems can be solved, that things can be better. Not in a foolish or unrealistic way, but in a way that creates hope and confidence among the people. For without that hope and confidence, there can be no end to conflict.

The second need is for a clear and determined policy not to yield to the men of violence. Over and over they have tried to destroy the peace process in Northern Ireland and, at times, they have nearly succeeded. Last July, after the agreement was reached and had been approved in referendum, three young Catholic boys were burned to death as they slept in their beds. As you all know, in August, the devastating bomb in Omagh killed twenty-nine people and injured more than three hundred people, Catholic and Protestant alike. These were acts of appalling hatred and ignorance and must be totally condemned. But to succumb to the temptation to retaliate would be to give the criminals what they want – a return to sectarian conflict. The only way to deal with such actions is to bring those responsible swiftly to justice and to go forward in peace. Backing peace requires an endless supply of perseverance and patience and understanding. Sometimes, and often for me in Northern Ireland, the mountains seemed so high and the rivers so wide that it was hard to continue the journey, but, no matter how doubtful, the search for peace must go on. Seeking an end to conflict is not for the timid or for the tender; it takes courage and steady nerves in the face of violence.

The third need is a willingness to compromise. Peace and political stability cannot be achieved in a sharply divided society, unless there is a genuine willingness to understand the other point of view and to enter into principled compromise. That's easy to say, but very hard to do, because it requires political leaders to take risks for peace. Most political leaders dislike risk-taking of any kind. They become political leaders by avoiding risks and minimizing risks and so to ask them in politically difficult and personally dangerous circumstances to take risks for peace is asking much, but, it must be asked and they must respond. It is one of the curious paradoxes of human history that, in time of war, political leaders can, and indeed do, take the most desperate gamble, but, in time of peace, there is a reluctance, a timidity, a fearfulness that restrains their actions. I know it can happen because I saw it first hand in Northern Ireland. Men and women, some of whom had never before met, had never before spoken, had lived their entire political lives in hostility and conflict, came together and reached an agreement for peace. Admittedly, it was difficult, admittedly there are now problems with implementation, but it did happen and if it can happen there, it can happen anywhere.

A fourth principle is to recognize that implementation of agreements is often more difficult and always more important

than reaching them. Sometimes these agreements are so difficult to reach. In Northern Ireland, we had negotiations for
two years. But as we've seen in Northern Ireland, as we've seen
in the Middle East, as we've seen in the Balkans, getting
implementation is even more difficult. This leads me directly
to Northern Ireland at the present time. I've just come from
Belfast where I have spent the last several days. During my
time there, I met with the political leaders of all of the parties
who supported the Agreement. No one can say for certain
that peace in Northern Ireland will endure. This is a particularly tense period involving the continuing problems of
decommissioning and its relationship with the formation of
the executive. Reports will be received in the coming months
from independent commissions on policing and criminal justice and each poses a threat to the continuing stability of the
process. In combination, they may, in the end, bring the
Agreement down. But I believe that the Agreement will
endure. I believe that peace can be made permanent and that
political stability can be achieved. I look at the following facts:
the guns have been largely silent for two years; still they have
not been entirely silent and one political murder is one too
many. However, the people have paid for peace and they don't
want to go back to the troubles. The decisions there now
involve all those parties who supported the Agreement. Those
opposed to Agreement, both within and without the political
spectrum, have tried mightily over the last eighteen months to
prevent and then derail the Agreement, and they have failed.
The future of the Agreement now rests in the hands of those
parties who support it. It would not only be an immense
tragedy, it would be an almost insensible irony, if the process
now failed because those who took the huge step of reaching
agreement fell out over its interpretation. The Northern

Ireland Assembly is in existence for the first time; they don't yet have authority; hopefully they will in just a few weeks. The parties now talk directly and regularly. In the two years of the negotiations David Trimble and Gerry Adams never once spoke; they communicated through me as chairman. Yesterday, I sat in Belfast at a press conference between the two of them; they spoke easily, as they have now done for many months. What was once impossible is now routine and not even worthy of comment. And finally I think, and most importantly, it is as true today as it was on that Good Friday, that the alternative to this Agreement could be unprecedented. As we entered the final hours of the long negotiating process, I reminded the delegates of what they had so often told me – that if this process failed and sectarian conflict was the result, it would be on a scale far wider and far more deadly than ever before. I told them that if that happened, they, the political leaders, would be found accountable by history. That is even truer now. History might have forgiven the failure to reach an agreement, since few thought it possible, but history will never understand or forgive the failure to implement the Agreement, once reached by the parties who got together on Good Friday. And so I think that, in the end, they will be able to reach an agreement on implementation and move forward, and I hope and pray that it happens soon.

There is another principle that existed in Northern Ireland, that extends beyond conflict situations, but I think it's so important that it's worth mentioning. I recall clearly my first day in Northern Ireland four and half years ago. In the morning, I was taken to a meeting on the Nationalist side of the peace line – a thirty-foot high wall, topped in places with barbed wire which physically separates two communities in Belfast. I had lived in Berlin for some time and was familiar with the Berlin Wall, but nothing prepared me for the shock of seeing the Peace Line – one of the most depressing man-made structures I've ever observed – a visible ongoing testimony to the length, intensity and bitterness of this conflict. And that was on the Nationalist side. Then in the afternoon, I had a profitable meeting on the Unionist side with a group of Protestants, which included the local vicars, community activists and development officers. Although they had no communication co-ordination, to my surprise they delivered a salutary message. In the urban areas of Belfast, on both sides of the line, there was a high correlation between unemployment and violence. They told me that as many as one out of two males in the urban areas of Northern Ireland, are born, live their lives and die, without ever having held a job, and without ever having the prospects of getting a job. Now, of course, the conflict in Northern Ireland is not exclusively or even primarily economic – it involves deep roots of religious and national identity – but there is an economic factor. I was told that where there is no hope, where there is no opportunity, people are more willing to turn to violence. As I sat and listened to them, I thought I could just as easily be sitting in Chicago, or any major American city, or Calcutta, or Johannesburg, or any major city in the world. This fear and lack of opportunity is the fuel for conflict and instability everywhere. Hope, a chance to prosper, is the best way to solve every political problem including the potential for instability. Aspirations of people everywhere are the same: to have a decent job; to earn enough income to support one's family and to get children off to a good start in life in a safe and secure environment; and to have the psychological feeling of doing something meaningful in and with our lives.

I'm not objective; I'm equally biased in favour of all of the people of Northern Ireland. Having spent nearly four years among them, I have come to like and admire them very much. They have faults, they're quick to take offence, they argue at the drop of a hat and talk all night, but they're also warm and generous, energetic and productive. They've made mistakes, but they're learning from them. Some, not all, agree that violence won't solve their problems; some, not all, agree that Unionists and Nationalists have more in common than that which divides them. They all know that knowledge of history is a good thing but being chained to the past is not. There are going to be many setbacks along the way, but I believe that the direction is firmly and finally set. The people of Ireland, North and South, overwhelmingly in referendum, in a free, open and democratic election approved the Agreement.

When that Agreement was reached, it was about six o'clock on Good Friday of last year. We had been in negotiations for two years and continuously for the previous two days and nights. I hadn't slept for nearly forty hours and we were all exhausted but elated. As we gathered for the last time, extremely emotional, I told the delegates that, for me, the Good Friday Agreement was the realization of a dream which had sustained me through the most difficult three and a half days of my life. Now that we had accomplished the agreement, I told them I had another dream, it was this: my dream is to return to Northern Ireland in a few years with my young son, travel round that beautiful country and look at one of the spectacular landscapes on earth and feel the warmth of the people. Then, on one rainy afternoon, we'll drive to Stormont and go to the Northern Ireland Assembly, where we'll sit in the visitor's gallery and we'll quietly watch and listen as the members of that Assembly face the ordinary issues of life in a democratic society: education and healthcare, tourism and fisheries. There will be no talk of war for the war will have long been over. There will be no talk of peace for peace will be taken for granted. And on that day, the day on which peace is taken for granted in Northern Ireland, I will be truly fulfilled.

8 July 1999

1   US First Lady, Hillary Rodham Clinton, signs the Visitors' Book at NUI, Galway, as University President, Dr Patrick F. Fottrell, looks on.

2   Dr Garret Fitzgerald, Chancellor of National University of Ireland,
    and US First Lady, Hillary Rodham Clinton, on her visit to
    NUI, Galway on 12 May 1999.

3   US First Lady, Hillary Rodham Clinton, delivers her lecture 'Our
Obligations to Each Other: Continuing the Quest for Peace', the
first lecture in the Millennium Lectures Series.

4   Hillary Rodham Clinton, US First Lady, in the academic procession with Dr Patrick F. Fottrell, President NUI, Galway, and Dr Garret Fitzgerald, Chancellor NUI, after she was awarded with a degree of Doctor of Laws *honoris causa* by the University.

5   Before delivering her millennium lecture, United Nations High
Commissioner for Human Rights, Mary Robinson, shares a
light moment with with (l–r) Dr Patrick F. Fottrell, President of
NUI, Galway, Professor Ruth Curtis, Vice-President for
Development & External Affairs, and Professor James Ward,
Vice-President for Human & Physical Resources.

6   UN High Commissioner for Human Rights, Mary Robinson, delivers her oration 'Human Rights at the Dawn of the New Millennium', the second lecture in the Millennium Lecture Series.

7   UN High Commissioner for Human Rights, Mary Robinson, answers questions from the audience after delivering her lecture at NUI, Galway.

8   US Senator George Mitchell and Dr Patrick F. Fottrell, University
President, pictured in the Quadrangle, NUI, Galway on 8 July 1999.

9   Senator George Mitchell delivers his lecture, 'Making Peace', on 8 July 1999.

10 University President, Dr Patrick F. Fottrell, presents US Senator George Mitchell with a replica of *Twin Spires*. Also pictured is sculptor John Behan.

11 Nobel Laureate, Seamus Heaney, pictured on his visit to
NUI, Galway on 16 September 1999, with University President,
Dr Patrick F. Fottrell.

12 Seamus Heaney, Nobel Laureate, on his visit to NUI, Galway in 1999, shares a joke with Dr Séamus MacMathúna, Rúnaí na hOllscoile.

13 Seamus Heaney, Nobel Laureate, delivers his millennium lecture '*Us* as in *Versus*: Poetry and the World'.

14 NUI, Galway President, Dr Patrick F. Fottrell, introduces Commander William Leslie King, great grandson of Professor William King, who was Professor of Mineralogy, Geology, and Natural History in the University, 1849–83, to Her Excellency Mrs Mary McAleese, Uachtarán na hÉireann, at the Gala Banquet, 31 October 1999.

15 Pictured at the Gala Banquet at NUI, Galway on 31 October 1999,
were Mary Dooley, Bursar, Dr Martin McAleese, Professor Iognáid
Ó Muircheartaigh, Registrar, Her Excellency Mrs Mary McAleese,
Uachtarán na hÉireann, Dr Patrick F. Fottrell, President of
NUI, Galway, Professor Ruth Curtis, Vice-President, Professor
James Ward, Vice-President, and Dr Séamus Mac Mathúna, Rúnaí
na hOllscoile.

16 Her Excellency Mary McAleese, Uachtarán na hÉireann, delivers her keynote speech at the Gala Banquet at NUI, Galway on 31 October 1999.

Us as in *Versus*:
Poetry and the World

Seamus Heaney, Nobel Laureate

The year two thousand. The millennium. The words stir us, perhaps because they are proof that we can hold our own against the infinite. They help us to 'cage the minute', as Louis MacNeice said, and yet they also tempt us to let the minute out of its cage. There is a kind of sublime promise in them. When we hear somebody say 'millennium', we don't think immediately of its mathematical or historiographical significance. The fact that we are marking the two thousandth anniversary of the birth of Christ is not the first thing that springs to mind. Nothing as precise. The word prompts us rather to be on the alert for some vast meaning hovering just out of reach; it makes us wish we could apprehend it more satisfactorily and give it a more articulate or contemplatable form; and it makes us realize that even if we drink all the champagne in the world on 31 December 1999, we will never altogether match the sense of occasion which the date entails.

It was obviously in the hope of rising to the occasion with something more intellectually nutrient than a bottle of bubbly that the university organized these lectures and invited a poet to deliver one of them. Poetry, after all, is an art which can tie down things that are aspiring and cloudy and tether them in the ground of our immediate experience. In my own case, for example, those words, 'the year two thousand', open

[49]

a space that corresponds to my memory of a high, bright, ionized space of air standing above the weir at Toomebridge in
Co. Antrim, at a spot where the waters of Lough Neagh flow
down into the broad stream of the Lower Bann. Every time I
went there as a child, I had a sensation of revelation, as if the
sky above the weir were an archway to the infinite. And nowadays in my imagination the word 'millennium' stands open
and shines with the same kind of brightness. What all this
proves, I think, is something that I will be arguing later on,
namely, that our best way of confronting great realities may be
to look for a reflection of them in realities that are nearer
home. We can discover important meanings for ourselves by
gazing with attention into the deep, clear mirror of analogy.
And the deepest and clearest mirror of all is to be found in
poetry. This lecture, therefore, will be about the way poetry
reflects the world; but I will also have something to say about
the responsibilities which universities have in relation to the
poetic heritage and the humanist heritage in general.

I have long been interested in the way poetry performs
when it is, as we say, up against it, and this is one of the senses in which the word *versus* figures in the title. *Versus* is, of
course, a Latin term, with an ancient lineage behind it, but it
is far from being a learned term. Fifty years ago, for example,
it figured in the football supporters' vocabulary, giving a kind
of classical stamp of approval to the local life – 'St Malachy's
versus O'Donovan Rossa's, at the County Grounds, Magherafelt' – and in that context the term carried with it, as it still
does, a sense of both promise and contest, of a performance
to be conducted openly and strenuously.

Poetry too is called upon to be a protagonist in the public
arena, to answer back with its clear tongue when the world
gets muddied and bloodied. Poetry *versus* tyranny, poetry

versus injustice, poetry *versus* war: it has been the destiny of
the art in this century to be involved over and over again in
these struggles. In the draft introduction of his *Collected
Poems*, for example, written shortly before he was killed at the
Western Front in 1918, Wilfred Owen revealed the demands
that poetry would place upon its representatives in the
decades to come, often with tragic consequences: 'All a poet
can do today is warn,' Owen famously declared. 'That is why
the true Poets must be truthful.' And forty years later, under
moral and intellectual siege in a different part of Europe, the
Polish poet Zbnigiew Herbert would write that the task of the
poet was 'to salvage out of the catastrophe of history at least
two words, without which all poetry is an empty play of
meanings and appearances, namely: justice and truth'. So the
phrase '*us* as in *versus*' was meant to convey the idea that when
we find ourselves up against it, at moments of extreme crisis
in either the political or the private life, poetry becomes a nec-
essary human resource.

What I want to do here, therefore, is to reaffirm the value
of that resource by considering how one famous poem from
the past worked for its original audience and how it contin-
ued to work for audiences down to our own day. Then, in
order to show how the old poem is still alive and well two
thousand years after it was written, I'll give an account of how
it helped me to write a poem of my own about conditions in
contemporary Ireland at this millennial moment. I'll therefore
be reading from both poems and will end the lecture with
some general reflections, illustrated once again by reference to
a couple of poems by other Irish writers.

I've talked about the adversarial meaning of the word
versus, but first and foremost *versus* signifies a 'turn', so, I'd
now like to remind you of two different senses of 'turn' that

relate to my concerns in this lecture. First of all, there is the turn in time evoked by the word 'millennium', and secondly, there is the turn which is indicated when we employ the English word 'verse' – the turn, that is, which occurs at the end of a line of poetry, and which we unconsciously acknowledge when we speak of a line being 'well-turned'.

A line of verse is a unit that must hold together for both the eye and the ear. You can recognise verse merely by noticing the shape of the lines on the page. Unlike prose, which runs from one margin to the next indiscriminately, and can be set by a printer in all kinds of different arrangements without affecting its intrinsic rhythms, verse must be set in the same way each time. Whatever size of print is used, the integrity of the individual line-length has to be respected. This is because the break at the end of the line is functional rather than arbitrary: verse is not, as they say, chopped prose. The way the line turns is a factor in how it is going to be heard. It helps to score the poem for performance by the voice, whether the voice is that of a silent reader or someone speaking the poem aloud. Sometimes the turn is as regular as a sentry's pacing his beat, as in W.B. Yeats' famous instructions to Irish poets, where every move is sharply marked off and efficiently executed:

> Irish poets, learn your trade.
> Sing whatever is well made.
> Scorn the sort now growing up,
> All out of shape from toe to top,
> Their unremembering hearts and heads
> Base born product of base beds.

No mistaking where the turns come in that passage. Or where they come in the beautiful measured ending of Andrew

Marvell's poem, 'The Bermudas', where a group of English puritans are imagined singing hymns as they row across the ocean to found a new colony in the South Atlantic. Marvell's poem concludes:

> Thus sang they in the English boat
> An holy and a cheerful note;
> And all the way, to guide their chime,
> With falling oars they kept the time.

The rowing analogy is a very good one for what happens in traditional verse. In order to propel himself and his craft forward, the oarsman must sit facing backward. In a similar fashion, the poet's craft requires the poet to take cognizance of all the poetry that lies behind him in order to devise another way forward. The poet must keep his future-oriented intelligence fully informed by the steadfastness of his backward look, scanning what has gone before the better to plot what to do in and for the future. Our cultural inheritance, in other words, is not a backlog but a launching pad, and the literature of the past is full of creative potential. Like the angel of history who, as Walter Benjamin said, is dragged into the future while staring directly into the past, the angel of poetry is also subject to strains that compel him in both directions.

Great original works which open new possibilities for the art are often deeply dependent on previous masterpieces. We need only think of Virgil's relationship with Homer, and then of Dante's relationship with Virgil, to be reminded of the reality and the radiance of this phenomenon, although the interdependence between what *has* been written and what will *get* written is evident in more familiar and less exalted works. Take, for example, the opening line of W.B. Yeats' 'The Lake

Isle of Innisfree'. 'I will arise and go now and go to Innisfree,' said Yeats, far off in London, dreaming of his mother's home landscape in Cu. Sligo. 'I will arise and go to my father's house,' said the prodigal son, in the New Testament parable. Whether Yeats intended the echo or his reader is fully alert to it does not lessen its reality, nor the reality of the underground cable that runs deep in the language and connects the two utterances.

When it comes to language and our susceptibility to it, we are extraordinarily well equipped. Something goes to work beneath our conscious awareness, something which nevertheless derives from and depends upon the mental possessions we acquire as intelligent inhabitants of human history and culture. Our cultural equipment, in fact, is every bit as complex and as sensitive as our physical equipment, and just as our bodily sense of hearing is an evolved system for keeping us alive and alert as creatures of the planet, so too our cultural antennae are a development that helps to locate us in the zone of consciousness. Indeed, one way of describing the heritage of poetry would be to call it a sounding line or an evolutionary tree of consciousness. Us as in *versus*, so to speak. But I'm getting ahead of myself.

I want to talk not only about the turn of the poetic line and the ongoing strength of poetic tradition. I also want to relate these things to the millennial turn of time that we are here to contemplate, and that is why I'm now going to spend some time with a poem that has been regarded for centuries as one of the great visionary poems in the European tradition. It was written on the very threshold of the first millennium of our era and has within it an apocalyptic yearning that guarantees its appeal to readers standing on threshold of the third. It is about a historical turn from bad to better times, about the arrival of a new age, one in which long-held hopes of a peaceful future are about to be fulfilled. And according to the poet, this longed-for change in the world's affairs is going to be ushered in by the birth of a child. At one stage the poet – Publius Virgilius Maro, known to us today simply as Virgil – addresses him in the womb and says:

> The time has come about at last for you
> To take upon you those great honours foretold;
> Behold how the vaulted universe trembles in awe –
> Earth and the range of sea and depth of sky –
> Glorying in the new age coming in.

This is one of those unusual things, a prophecy that is not doom-laden, and its hopeful register and benign vistas recall other great visions of redeemed time. The child in these lines appears like the child in Isaiah, so it was hard for later Christian commentators not to identify him with the infant Jesus:

> Why then, said Isaias, listen to me, you that are of David's house ... Sign you ask none but sign the Lord shall give you. Maid shall be with child, and shall bear a son that shall be called Emmanuel. On butter and honey shall be this thriving. (Isaiah, 8: 13-15)

The biblical passage does harmonize most appositely with the Latin poem, and the fact that the poem also identifies the arrival of the new age with the reappearance on earth of a Virgin would further encourage Christian readers to identify the fruit of her womb with Christ, and to identify the new race that was due to appear with those baptized in the Christian faith. In Christian homiletics, Mary was the new Eve and the fact that the Latin poem envisages the transformed world as one in which the serpent will be destroyed only served to confirm this equation of the figures in the poem with the central figures in the Judaeo-Christian story.

The date of the poem's composition, moreover, seemed to confirm its prophetic status. It was known to have been written some forty years before Christ's birth and so, in the Middle Ages, it was read by the learned as a prediction of the Incarnation. To those commentators who pored over the ancient texts for their hidden significances, the fact that the poem was written in Rome rather than Judea and that its author was a Latin poet rather than a Hebrew prophet was no deterrent to their understanding of it as inspired utterance. In the language of today, the Christians appropriated it. If any historical objections did present themselves, they could always be quelled by supposing that Virgil, himself a learned man, had studied Isaiah and other related Messianic writings. The commentators read his apostrophe to the little child as if it were the outcry of a Roman Simeon:

> *Aspice convexo nutantem pondere mundum,*
> *Terrasque tractusque maris caelumque profundum;*
> *Aspice, venturo laetentur ut omnia saeclo!*
> *O mihi tum longae maneat pars ultima vitae,*
> *Spiritus et quantum sat erit tuae dicere facta.*

'O then,' say those last lines, addressing the child, 'let me live out the final part of my long life and have breath enough and spirit enough to tell about the things you have done.' The

sense of an ending, the promise of a history about to be transformed, is both unmistakable and mysterious. The poem is
capable of speaking to people's yearnings at the end of the second millennium every bit as suggestively as it spoke on the eve
of the first, and when I read it recently in a new translation by
the American poet David Ferry, it wakened my interest in all
kinds of vivid and unexpected ways.

This was partly because a young woman I know in
Northern Ireland is due to have a baby early in the year 2000
and Virgil's poem brought her suddenly and sweetly into my
mind. And it brought too a twinge of creative joy, one of those
moods when, as Robert Frost says, a poem begins in delight.
I had a premonition of how I might get started on a millennium poem. Needless to say, many invitations to compose
such a poem have been flying around in the past few months;
it's an obvious commission and one that a poet could hardly
help setting himself. But the prophetic role is a daunting one
and anyhow, when it comes to poetry, you can hardly ever get
to grips with public themes directly. You need to discover
some personal matter that you can dig through in your own
way, in order to come out public on the other side. At any
rate, once I connected the baby in the northern womb with
the baby in Virgil's poem and further connected the pair of
them to the mood of expectancy and anxiety that has prevailed in Northern Ireland in the aftermath of the Good Friday
Agreement, the poem got under way. And it was greatly assist-
ed by the fact that an eclipse of the sun had occurred around
that time, adding to the sense of omen and possibility.

In the standard commentary on Virgil's *Eclogues*, Wendell
Clausen makes it clear that the fourth poem is less a prophe-
cy than a response to contemporary political conditions in
Rome in the year 40 BC. This was as uncertain a time for the

citizens of Italy as the present time is for citizens of Northern Ireland. The wars that had begun in the wake of the assassination of Julius Caesar were not quite over. The triumvirate of Marc Antony, Lepidus and Octavian had defeated the forces Brutus and Cassius at Phillippi, but the final curtain had not fallen on that violent period of Roman history. The Battle of Actium, when Octavian would defeat Antony and initiate the Pax Romana, was still to come. It was not yet the moment of what Virgil would call *pacatum orbem*, the world at peace. At the moment of the poem's composition, in fact, Octavian and Antony were dividing their spheres of influence in the Roman territories between them. Antony was taking command in the east and Octavian in the west, an arrangement known to history as the Pact of Brundisium, and this pact was solemnized, as Clausen says, 'in the high Roman fashion, as Antony took to wife Octavian's sister, the blameless Octavia'. And so, Clausen continues, there was no mystery about the child:

> To contemporary [that is, the original Roman] readers, the vexed question 'Who is the boy?' would not have occurred. They knew well enough who was meant: the expected son of Antony and Octavia and heir to Antony's greatness – the son that never was …

In our own time and place, as in Virgil's, there is a feeling that some respite from violence is due, that the old warring factions have worked themselves into a situation where a new political structure is the only way forward. Then as now, peace suddenly presented itself on the one hand as a frail possibility and on the other as the only path for all parties to pursue. Everybody was (and is) simultaneously weary to death and fearful of giving up hope. So it became obvious that Virgil and I had something to talk about, and I wrote a Bann Valley Eclogue, where he and I, as farmer's sons who have entered the swim of poetry, talk across two millennia. I'll read you just a few stanzas, to give a taste of the whole thing:

Poet   Bann Valley muses, give us a song worth singing,
        Something that rises like the curtain in
        Those words *And it came to pass* and *In the beginning.*
        Help me to please my hedge-schoolmaster Virgil
        And the child that's due. Maybe, heavens, sing
        Better times for her and her generation

Virgil Here are my words you'll have to find a place for:
        Carmen, ordo, nascitur, saeculum, gens.
        Their gist in your tongue and province should be clear
        Even at this stage. Poetry, order, the times,
        The nation, wrong and renewal, then an infant birth
        And a flooding away of all the old miasma …

Poet   *Pacatum orbem:* your words are too much nearly,
        Even 'orb' by itself. What on earth could match it?
        And then, last month, mid-morning, the wind
            dropped,
        A millennial chill, birdless and dark, prepared,
        A firstness steadied, a lastness, a born awareness
        As name dawned into knowledge: I saw the orb.

Virgil Eclipses won't be for this child. The cool she'll know
        Will be the pram hood over her vestal head.
        Big dog daisies will get fanked up in the spokes.

She'll lie on summer evenings listening to
A chug and slug going on in the milking parlour.
Let her never hear close gunfire or explosions ...

I said at the beginning that the university had arranged this
series of lectures in response to a need we all feel as we
approach the millennium, a need to make sense of the aura
that surrounds the very word. In addressing this need, the
university is fulfilling its proper function; it is attempting to
enlarge and refine our understanding by asking us to search
out and take possession of the sum of our knowledge and then
to re-search it, press upon it in order to make it yield up further meanings. In my contribution to the series, therefore, it
seemed worthwhile to insist upon the value of one area of
knowledge that has accrued to us over the past two thousand
years, namely, the literary heritage itself. This is only one part
of the whole humanist culture which the university has in its
care, but it is a crucial part, and a part that must be preserved
and revalued as vigorously in the twenty-first century as it was
in the first.

One of the reasons we need literature is because it is a
source of images which have an inner inevitability and a sure
claim on our understanding as a source of possible meanings.
And I take some of the key words in that sentence from the
Italian writer, Italo Calvino, from a book that consists of five
brilliant chapters but which is entitled *Six Memos for the Next
Millennium.* The discrepancy is explained by the fact that
Calvino died before he had completed the work, which was to
be a series of six lectures for delivery at Harvard in 1985.
Essentially these were personal meditations on literature, quo-
tations from texts that he loved, and commentaries on them.
The point of the whole exercise was to commend certain qual-

ities which he thought should continue to be valued in the next millennium, qualities to which he gave the names lightness, quickness, exactitude, visibility and multiplicity. It was in the chapter on 'Exactitude' that I found the following paragraph:

> Consider visual images, for example. We live in an unending rainfall of images. The most powerful media transform the world into images and multiply it by means of the phantasmagoric play of mirrors. These are images stripped of the inner inevitability that ought to mark every image as form and as meaning, as a claim on the attention and as a source of possible meanings. Much of this cloud of visual images fades at once, like the dreams that leave no trace in the memory, but what does not fade is the feeling of alienation and discomfort ... this lack of substance ... My discomfort arises from the loss of form that I notice in life, which I try to oppose with the only weapon I can think of – the idea of literature.

To put it another way, then. If the work of calculating time is, as I suggested earlier, a way of holding our own against the infinite, the image – the poem, the work of literature – is a way of holding our own against the inchoate and the insubstantial. Because of its form, it works against that dissolution which Calvino speaks of. Everything does indeed flow, and the most concentrated mind may indeed be little more than 'a long-legged fly upon the stream', but we would not have the pleasure of grasping even that much reality as satisfactorily as we do had not Heraclitus thought of the course of events as a stream and had not W.B. Yeats thought of the attentive mind as a fly on the face of it – had they not, in other words, thought in images, and had the scholars and teachers who came after them not saved and valued those images, and disseminated them.

Here is another writer saying much the same thing in a different way. This passage occurs in the introduction to Stanislaw Baranczak's recent anthology of Polish poetry from the second half of the twentieth century, including work by that Zbigniew Herbert whom I mentioned at the beginning. 'As a rule,' Baranczak writes,

> there is an intermediary between society's experience and the individual's psyche – a kind of go-between that can be called culture. If not for that, the outer world of facts and events and the inner world of language and feelings and thoughts would resemble two interlocutors speaking different languages with no way to communicate. It is precisely culture that serves as an interpreter – an interpreter who helps us to understand what reality tells us and what it asks us about, and who, at the same time, helps us to formulate our own questions in a comprehensive language of symbols.
>
> Within culture perhaps the most apt interpreter of this kind is poetry.

Poetry is indeed important, but as a vehicle of culture, the university too is a vital and functioning entity, and one of its functions is to keep those interpretive skills which Baranczak attributes to culture as honed and up to the mark as possible. Cultural memory is not a burden but a source of liberation and renewal, and Polish poets know better than most how the inheritance of the classical past can reinforce the spirit of hope and endurance in a difficult present. In the repressive atmosphere and police-state conditions that prevailed in Poland during the days of the Warsaw Pact, stories of the gods and heroes and great historical figures of the Greek and Roman past were reinterpreted by artists and intellectuals living under pressure. The stories offered a way of contending with the totalitarian state. The classical images still retained what Dr Johnston would have called 'the stability of truth'; in the words of Calvino, they had an inner inevitability and a claim on the attention as a source of possible meanings.

But it was not only in Warsaw Pact countries that poets had recourse to the heritage of the past in order to facilitate the all-important dialogue between the outer world of facts and events and the inner world of feelings and thoughts. In our own distressful country, in the middle of this century, the Northern Irish poet John Hewitt turned to classical times in order to take the measure of his own times. By doing so, Hewitt discovered that he could bring his individual psyche into relationship with his society's experience and as a result he was able to write his historically important poem 'The Colony'. He found a way of holding his own against his own inner confusion – a confusion induced by his devotion, on the one hand, to the British cultural inheritance and the Protestant religious tradition of the north, and by his sympathy, on the other, for the excluded status of the Irish Catholic nationalist minority within the Union – a Union which he nevertheless still favoured. In the poem, Hewitt imagined himself a Roman colonist who had stayed on in some outpost of the Roman Empire after the legions left, a colonist separate from the natives by reason of history, sympathetic to them because of the way they had been expropriated, and yet delib-

erately insisting on his ongoing right to the confiscated land
which the Romans had once granted him. By drawing this
analogy Hewitt not only provided himself with an interpretive device that helped him to understand what reality was
telling him, he also managed to do the same for his readers.

Moreover, since we are in Galway, *agus ó's rud é gur coláiste
ghaelach a b'eadh an choláiste seo le blianta,* I think that another obvious truth is worth emphasizing. This is surely the place
and the time to insist that the Irish heritage has been and
remains an indispensable resource and value, a dream bank as
well as a data bank, one that will continue to be drawn upon
by poets and writers as they search out 'those images that
yet/Fresh images beget.' Or perhaps the heritage should be
likened to a tinder box rather than a dream bank, one in
which, to quote some other delightfully suggestive words of
Calvino, 'the spark ... shoots out from the collision of words
and new circumstances.' What, for example, could be artisti-
cally sturdier, more psychologically honest and more mytho-
logically grounded than Thomas Kinsella's poem, 'Remembering Old Wars'? In it, the private story of a marriage that is
being tested and strained appears as an aspect of the beautiful,
archetypal story of Cuchulain and Ferdia at the ford, loving
kinsmen honour-bound to fight to the death, to wound by
day and to bind their wounds by night. In Kinsella's poem,
the new circumstance is indeed richly and strangely illumi-
nated by sparks from the old words: the struggle within a contemporary marriage becomes an aspect of the combat between
Iron Age warriors. And vice-versa:

> What clamped us together? When each night fell we lay down
> In the smell of decay and slept, our bodies leaking,
> Limp as the dead, breathing that smell all night.

[64]

Then light prodded us awake, and adversity
Flooded up from inside us as we laboured upright
Once more to face the hells of circumstance.

And so on, without hope of change or peace.
Each dawn, like lovers recollecting their purpose,
We would renew each other with a savage smile.

In this poem, a scene from a warrior epic coalesces with a consciousness typical of the age of Beckett. The nine lines are in themselves sufficient proof that the cultural heritage contains elements essential to that symbolic language which allows us to get a perspective on our experience. New life streams from the old sources. It is, moreover, because of attention to those sources and constant re-interpretation of their meaning within the humanist disciplines of the university – it is because of this ongoing work of the academy that something like a shared idiom is still possible. Yet these disciplines are in danger of being slighted in favour of the new technological culture which Italo Calvino was describing, a culture that can speed up the supply and exchange of information to a dizzying and virtually miraculous degree, but can never quite supply a perspective on the dazzle it produces.

The sheer mass and glitter of the new information technologies are overwhelming. In fact, looking into the World Wide Web is like looking directly at an eclipse of the sun: the experience is in danger of blinding the subject rather than illuminating him. What is required, therefore, is some equivalent of the pincard, something we can hold up while turning our back on the glare, something that lets through a picture of what is happening while at the same time preserving us from being merely dazzled and bewildered. Poetry, and the cultural heritage in general, is such an equivalent. Hold it up to reality and an image comes through that allows us to see ourselves and our world in a contemplatable light: us as in *versus*.

16 September 1999

Address on the Occasion of the 150th Anniversary Celebrations

Mary McAleese, Uachtarán na hÉireann

In his famous essay, 'The Idea of a University', John Henry Cardinal Newman had this to say:

> The general principles of any study you may learn by books at home; but the detail, the colour, the tone, the air, the life which makes it live in us, you must catch all these from those in whom it lives already.

At the very heart of his idea of a university was not the beautiful buildings, the great library, the range of textbooks, the passing of exams – but the human beings, the teachers, those people who have inspired generations of students with their knowledge and passion and commitment.

That quote is central to what we are celebrating – 150 years, not of the establishment of National University of Ireland, Galway, itself, but rather of the establishment of teaching here. That distinction is an important one, for even in these days of the Internet, when we are surrounded by information, the role of the teacher is as valid, perhaps even more important, than ever. For teaching at its best is not simply about imparting information, citing references, enabling students to pass their exams. It is concerned to a far greater extent with unlocking the potential and imagination of a young student.

And we should never underestimate the potential that such an experience has in terms of transforming young – and sometimes not so young – lives. I do not mean that lives are changed in an instantaneous, dramatic way – I am sure that the experience of most lecturers is that the number of Pauline-like conversions is greatly outweighed by the students. But those students who have been fortunate enough to have had a university lecturer who stretched them intellectually, who taught them not how to learn, but how to think, to question, to seize opportunities, to have a sense of curiosity, of purpose and of determination – those are the individuals who have received the best possible education and the best possible preparation for life. They are the ones who will ultimately succeed, no matter what career path they choose; they are the ones who will become the leaders and 'doers' of tomorrow, the people who shape the world around them, the people that our society needs more than ever. And many graduates of this university have indeed achieved outstanding success in the public sector, business world and cultural sphere of this society and beyond.

Those generations of students, past and present, at this university are indeed blessed to have had the privilege of encountering so many Professors and lecturers who cared so deeply about what they taught and about the people they taught. More often than not, that dedication and commitment may have gone unnoticed and unremarked, overshadowed by the unending cycle of lectures, research, meetings and exams. That day-to-day work is at the core of what this university is about. But every so often, I believe it is important to stop for a moment on evenings such as this, to remind ourselves of how much has been achieved here over the years, of accomplishments which have been painstakingly and quietly built up over the years and whose true extent is only apparent when we stop to reflect and take stock. The knowledge that what you do here is important and does make a difference is a vital source of energy for recharging your batteries, for overcoming the inevitable disappointments or setbacks that arise from time to time, for picking yourselves back up and facing a new day, a new year and a new generation of students with a renewed sense of enthusiasm and passion.

Sometimes it may seem that the fruits of your labour are in vain, that the love of learning, of intellectual discourse, of truth, of caring about knowledge as a value unto itself has been drowned out by utilitarian concerns: the points system, exam results, employment prospects.

Ní inniu ná inné a thosaigh daoine ag tuar bhás na scoláireachta. Chomh fada siar leis an seachtú aois déag bhí an file Dáibhí Ó Bruadair ag caoineadh imeacht na foghlama agus na scoláireachta Gaeilge, mar ba léir dó sin ag an am é. Ní gá dúinn ach amharc ar a mhór-chaoineadh 'D'Aithle na bhFileadh'.

> D'aithle na bhfileadh dár ionmhas éigse is iúl
> Is mairg do-chonnairc an chinniúin d'éirigh dúinn
> A leabhair ag titim i leimhe 's i léithe i gcúil
> Is ag macaibh na droinge gan siolla dá séadaibh rún.

Mar a bhain le ghúin an fhile ní raibh dóchas ar bith ann. Bhí siad ag féachaint ar shaibhreas an tsaoil a bhí acu ag imeacht le gaoth agus leis na huaisle Gaelacha a bhí mar phatrúin orthu ag dul thar chuan amach. Dar leo go raibh síolta grá don fhoghlaim agus don scoláireacht a bhí curtha acu ag stracailt i dtalamh a bhí seasc, tur, marbh. Nach mór an chúis iontais agus áthais agus sásaimh do Dháibhí Ó Bruadair saol Gaelach na hollscoile seo a fheiceáil dá mbeadh sé linn inniu.

Bheadh sé soiléir dó nach raibh an talamh chomh tur, seasc, marbh agus a shíl sé, ach gur tháinig an grá don fhoghlaim agus do scoláireacht na Gaeilge i mbláth go láidir, agus go bhfuil an Ghaeilge agus gach a mbaineann léi beo beathach san ollscoil seo atá curtha agaibh féin. Tiocfaidh bláth orthu i mbealaí agus in áiteanna nach dtig linn a shamhlú.

Is mór an méid atá déanta agus atá á dhéanamh ag an ollscoil seo ar son chaomhnú agus chothú na teanga Gaeilge. Is dlúth-chuid de shaol na hollscoile í an Ghaeilge, agus ní beag an tionchar atá ag an bheocht, an bheatha agus an úire a ghineann an ollscoil ar shaol na cathrach agus na tíre. Ní haon chomh-tharlúint é gurb í Gaillimh croílár thionscal na teilifíse Gaeilge agus na scannánaíochta, dhá ghné de shaol na Gaeilge a bhíonn ag tarraing ar bhrí na hollscoile seo. Is leor an fuinneamh atá faoin teanga anseo mar fhreagra ar na droghallóirí a bhíonn ag síor-thuar bhás na Gaeilge agus an chultúir atá mar dhlúth-chuid di.

Ba mhaith liom mo bhuíochas a chur in iúl don Dochtúir Fottrell agus don Dochtúir Ruth Curtis, atá ina ball de Comhairle an Stáit, do Sheán Mac Suibhne agus don choiste eagrúcháin a thug cuireadh dom bheith i láthair libh ar an ócáid stairiúil seo, ócáid cheiliúrtha céad caoga bliain de theagasc san ollscoil seo. Tá a fhios agam go bhfuil bhur gcuid pleananna féin agaibh chun an chéad caoga bliain eile de shaol na hollscoile a dhéanamh chomh rathúil agus chomh fiúntach agus chomh bríomhar leis an chéad go leith atá díreach imithe.

Guím gach rath agus séan oraibh san obair thábhachtach atá romhaibh amach, cur agus baint an eolais agus na foghlama.

Go n-éirí go geal libh. Go raibh maith agaibh.

30 Deireadh Fómhar 1999

[70]

Illustrations

Illustrations supplied by Aengus McMahon and Mike Shaughnessy.